Unfinished Poetry

Custom Books Publishing

© Copyright 2007 by Sean Holliday

Library of Congress Cataloging in Publication Data

ISBN   1434811212

9781434811219

Printed in the United States of America

For Heather

Contents

Unfinished Poetry

Sean Holliday

Preface to *Unfinished Poetry*

In the nightstand next to my bed is a Ninja Turtles folder. Its edges have been reinforced with nylon tape and, for its age, it is in remarkably good shape. I bought it approximately fifteen years ago; long after the Ninja Turtles had gone out of style (before they came back in) and years after I was far too old to be keeping my homework in a Ninja Turtles folder. (Those facts were the main motivation in buying it.) I think I used it for AP American History that year and, since I had reinforced the edges, AP English the next. Fifteen years later, when my kids are getting old enough to appreciate the Ninja Turtles, it serves as my "graveyard of unfinished poetry."

Sometimes a poem comes to you start-to-finish in a matter of minutes. Sometimes you carve it out word-by-word-by-word over a matter of days, weeks, months, or years. Sometimes you have a great idea or a couple of lines or simply a feeling and that's as far as you get before life pushes you in a different direction. It's those poems that I entrust to the safe-, nylon-tape-reinforced, keeping of Leonardo, Donatello, Raphael, and Michelangelo.

The poems in this collection do not represent those from the graveyard. (A collection of four-word thoughts, half-finished stanzas, and random scribbles would constitute a rather poor literary effort.) But several of the poems here did spend time there before being resuscitated and eventually completed. Others, that were never put on hold long enough to be handed over to the heroes in a half-shell, have been tweaked, re-worked or overhauled years after initially being considered done. Some may yet evolve. In that sense, the poems here may be unfinished. (I'm only the poet. I can't know for sure, at least not one hundred percent.) But for now, that's not the case.

The Ninja Turtles folder and its contents inspired the title poem. A myriad of other influences inspired the rest. I hope a few of the poems that follow will inspire you.

Sean Holliday

Preface to *Life in General*

I don't like poetry. Well, that's not true. I love poetry. I just don't understand it; at least not very well. In high school I had to do a report on Samuel Taylor Coleridge, including an oral analysis of The Sandpiper in front of the class. I don't remember what I said—I pretty much made it up anyway—but I got an A. Apparently the teacher was impressed. Of course she could have just been grading on a curve. Compared to the rest of the class, I was a regular Lord Byron. I, who couldn't recognize iambic pentameter if it hit me with a yard stick, was the best in the class at deciphering what those old dead guys were trying to say. It still annoyed me. Frustrated is a better word. I had to read each line 423 times and concentrate myself into an Excedrin-sized headache just to understand the surface of the poem's content. (The blatantly obvious hints that the teacher offered in an attempt to bridge the agonizing silence that inevitably followed any question of an analytical nature didn't hurt either.)

It was in those days of glassy-eyed classmates and stress-induced acne that I decided to publish a book of poetry that would emancipate AP English students all over the world from the bonds of ambiguity, verbosity and literary enigma that had enslaved them for centuries. I started with the title: 101 Poems that Rhyme. Then I wrote a non-rhyming poem. I decided rhyming was optional. Content, on the other hand, was not. Every poem, no matter what emotion it described, no matter what darkness it explored should end up-beat and positive; at least neutral. Then I wrote a poem that didn't. My position on the matter changed.

Over the years my philosophy of poetry has evolved. It probably will continue. Today I believe that a poem should be uplifting and edifying; at least insightful. It should be honest and sincere and should try to convey a message—not necessarily a moral—but it should communicate something: the beauty of a spring morning; the swelling joy of friendship; the best way to annoy your fellow commuters while stuck in an I-15 traffic jam. Without communication, what good are words?

Hopefully that's what sets these poems apart. I call them "everyday poems" because poemoftheday.com was taken, but also because they contain lines and ideas that I find myself using every day. They are written for everyday people in everyday situations. Some are clever and funny. Some are spiritual and uplifting. Some are thoughtful. Some are sad. Most can be understood on several levels and multiple readings are encouraged. But if you find yourself reading a particular poem for the 423rd time, hopefully it's to experience the depth of the writing, not just to scratch the surface. I hope that all of the poems in this book communicate the reason they were written; without the use of painkillers.

Sean Holliday

Unfinished Poetry

Welcome to the graveyard
Of unfinished poetry
What you are seeing
Are all of the thoughts, ideas and feelings
That never reached completion
On a finished page of poems

Once, these dusty, tattered words
Now tucked away and tabled
As partial and potential
Were masterpieces
Fresh and new
In the mind of the life-living poet
They were exciting and real
Alive and majestic
Full of all the things
That caused them to be written
And greatly loved
By the understanding soul
Of he who wrote them

But that was long ago
Time has forgotten them
To age and the moment
And now
Worn and wrinkled
Gray and fragile
They've returned to the graveyard
Of an ever-changing human heart
To await their inspiration
And another shot at greatness

On your left is a piece
From a rainy day in 1994
When the sheltered beliefs of night time
Were ravished by the light of day
Many dreams were challenged that afternoon
Heart strings were pulled
And tears were nearly shed
But the peaceful reality of evening
Restored beauty to the world
And only words were left behind
On your right you'll see
A profound little thought
First conceived in 1997
And standing ever since
Alone with nothing to follow
Deep and meaningful in its prime
It has now become old and faded
Almost forgotten
Still it continues hoping
That someday
Emotion will return again
And it will change the world
Perhaps it will

These few are just examples
Of the notes and types and titles
The words and whys and wonderings
That you'll find within the yard
Feel free to wander
And read as many as you like
Maybe as you peruse and ponder
You'll find a verse that speaks to you
And when you do
Then perhaps it too
Will accomplish what it's lived to do

Subject Matter

I read the words of poets heard
In times before my birth
Whose songs of love were sonnets of
The majesty of earth

And in reply I wonder why
Mine try to understand
To figure out and sing about
The majesty of man

The beauty known in worlds they've shown
Through imagery and rhyme
Has stood throughout the fear and doubt
And love and life of time

And shown God's hand in grains of sand
And bubbles of the sea
But failed to show His heart and soul
Ingrained in you and me

The songs of those who writing chose
To praise days one through five
Forget that on the next day's dawn
His image came to life

Creations of the Lord above
Though glorious and full
Are finished by the one that I
Examine and extol

Maybe

Maybe if I scribble long enough
These random lines of pencil lead
Will miraculously form words
And change the world
Or my world anyway
Maybe they'll relieve the stress
Of not being able to express myself
Not being able to say
What it is I want to say
Simply because I don't know
What it is I want to say
And scribbling
And scribbling
Until I decide
Because I know I want to say something

Waiting for inspiration to hit
Never works
Because it won't hit
Until you stop waiting
And then you won't have paper or a pencil
So, oh well
Maybe poetry was never meant to be put on paper
Sorry

A Rhyming Poem

Oh, no, no, no! See poems don't rhyme
At least the good ones won't
They haven't rhymed for quite some time
So when it comes to rhyming—don't

We need dark and dismal and really sad
And rhyming makes poems fun
We need something to say, "Man's really bad"
"And has been from day one"

I know. I know. You're young and free
And have never coped with stress
But life is just catastrophe
So catch up with the rest

If a poem doesn't change the world you see
Or at least give it a valiant try
Then it suffers from mediocrity
That's the way it is. I don't know why

Now go write something extremely tragic
Not beautiful garbage like this
Poems need reality; not all this magic
That's just the way life is

Gray Areas

In the darkness my words are hidden
In the bright of the sun they fade into nothingness
Can you understand these marks of heavy lead?
Or do they merely cross this page
On an endless track to oblivion?
My arm knots in an attempt
To loose the knot in my throat
But is it all in vain?
What will these words cause?
Will a life be touched?
Will a heart be mended?
Will a salty tear roll from any cheek but mine?
The lighting is perfect now
The words are clear
They have meaning
They have soul
But what's the forecast for tomorrow?

To Visualize Emotion

Thick and heavy fists of clay
Awkward in their motion
Got the notion anyway
To visualize emotion

Cumbersome and full of doubt
Slow and simple sketching
Took to stretching inside-out
Impressions that were etching

Humble hands of halting how
With hallowed hesitation
Witness their creation now
In reverent celebration

Different

Different
Equals second-rate
Equals inferior

Fresh
Equals amusing
Equals cute

New
Equals poor
Equals insignificant

Unique
Equals worthless
Equals bare

Everybody Seems to Like My Poetry

Everybody seems to like my poetry
And I guess I really don't know why
I mean, I try
But it's only the best I can do
And it's true
The words do come from the heart
The open part
And I try to describe the feeling
But it's such a feeble attempt

Everybody seems to like my poetry
Except sometimes the poet
I mean, he doesn't show it
But at times he knows there's more
And insecure
With the simplicity with which he writes
So plain and light
He wonders why he writes the way he does
But it's all that he knows how

Everybody seems to like my poetry
And so I keep on writing
Just deciding
That the words I choose may never be considered great
But some relate
To the things that I attempt to say
And someday
Maybe I will say enough
To know exactly why I said it

No Poetry

There just isn't poetry today
Don't know about tomorrow
I can't believe a tree had to give its life
For me to write those last two lines
What a waste

'Cause there just isn't poetry today
The last half hour proves it
And still I sit here writing
In the hopes of being wrong
Don't know why

There just isn't poetry today

Not an Ogden Nash Poem

Writing an Ogden Nash poem
While boarding a bus bound for home
Trying—against my nature—to avoid the use of rhythm
But words have rhythm in them
And songs that squire with them
Which is why
Though I try
As the bus passes by
I can't write an Ogden Nash poem

Words

Someone explained
That you couldn't feel words
And I wept at the things
That he said
Grammatically speaking
It was something I heard
But I heard with my heart
And my head

He said that a word
Was a thing of the ear
Just a thing
That gets placed in your mind
And the phrases he chose
Led to tissues and tears
But I guess
I'm just one of a kind

Rob and Og and Shel and I

Rob and Og and Shel and I
Set out to try and catch the sky
And from that partly-cloudy high
Relax and watch the world roll by

Shel dreamed of things we'd never seen
Rob saw the world in wakened dreams
Og pondered sleep and Listerine
I lingered somewhere in between

A Second Attempt at Ogden Nash Poetry

It really is very interesting to me:
this Nashian form of poetry.
While its subjects amuse me,
its meters confuse me.
I've never been able to rhyme without there following quite naturally a certain sense of rhythm.
(As I have expressed before, "…words have rhythm in them.")
Because of this, I find it extremely difficult to write a poem without meter.
And doing so now, I feel like a cheater.
But Nash created, embraced and mastered the technique,
publishing this new style in the New Yorker each week.
How he did it I will probably never understand.
For when it comes to rhyming without rhythm I am completely and unquestionably outmanned.
I don't mention this to in any way disparage Mr. Nash.
He is one of only three poets for whose work I have actually paid out cash.
I quite enjoy his words and rhymes.
And read aloud those I find most appealing to my wife and friends at times.
I've even learned to read them well;
consciously pausing after each sentence to allow the gist to gel.
But in efforts to date, I have not been able to duplicate his work.
Despite my best intentions, I find myself in a perpetual poetic Dunkirk.
As evidence I offer the above alliteration.
And resign this, my second attempt at Ogden Nash poetry, to eventual obliteration.
Progress, though—it must be said—has certainly been made.
And despite the use of meter here, I deem my homage paid.

Silencing The Critics

Monet informed Picasso
Your work is a fiasco

Picasso in a fury
Responded yours is blurry

Kandinsky told Cezanne
Your paintings make me yawn

Cezanne enlightened Klee
You ought to mimic me

Van Gogh abhorred Kandinsky
Dali and Da Vinci

Klee advised Van Gogh
Your art is just so so

Da Vinci, Dali, Kahlo
Were unimpressed with Warhol

Chagall found Kahlo hollow
And Dali hard to follow

Degas despised Renoir
Renoir reviled Degas

And Warhol deemed them all
As worthless as Chagall

And thus the brushes ceased
Monotony increased

Artistry deceased
And critics were appeased

Poems for Sale

Poems for sale
Who'll buy a poem?
They're not too expensive
You won't need a loan
They're perfect for work
Or school, church, or home
Poems for sale
Who'll buy a poem?

There are beautiful, dutiful, hootiful ones
Meaningful, dreamingful, seemingful ones
Some are beginning
And others are done
So who'll buy a poem?
Anyone?
Anyone?

Poems for sale
Fresh from the pen
They're not too confusing
Depressing or grim
But also not corny
Or shallow or thin
Poems for sale
Let the bidding begin

There are frantic, romantic, enchantical ones
Political, critical, witical ones
Some are for sorrow
And others for fun
So who'll buy a poem
Anyone?
Anyone?

Someone Else's Molehill

Be someone else's burden
You've been mine for too long
I'm strong enough to make it on my own
Alone without the herding
And dragging you along
To wrong me with the innocence you've shown

Be someone else's molehill
Her obstacle and climb
For I'm content to live without the view
And you're the kind of toil
That towers throughout time
And I'm too tired to tackle tasks like you

Be someone else's kite-string
Her anchor to the ground
I've found that falling freely feels like flight
And nights without a ceiling
Expose the sights and sounds
Of boundless beings hidden by the light

Be someone else's lover
I've no more love to give
I'll live my life with leisure when you're gone
And on my own discover
The life I could have lived
Forgiving faults forever on and on

Myopia Utopia

Myopia
Utopia
A wonderland of one

Augustean
Procrustean
Unique in unison

Monotonous
Forgottenous
With central sense of self

Dichotomy
Lobotomy
Commissioned off the shelf

Manic Mindy

Manic Mindy mulled the morrow
Over and again
And then again
And then again
And then again again

She weighed the sense against the sorrow
And opted to transcend
The things she'd been
Herself extend
But leave the friends she'd known till then

Not knowing how she'll do it now
And wondering if she should
She thinks about the options out
The couldn'ts that she could

Her heart contends with leaving friends
And questions wrong and right
Her head debates and speculates
And keeps her up at night

And wondering if the one she's with
Will ever be the one
She dreams of guys to analyze
When the journey here is done

The future there is only air
Without a guarantee
The past she loves is memories of
The girl she planned to be

The choice she made was over-weighed
Deep down she knows it's right
But doubts and fears and hidden tears
Confuse the conscious sight

And so she manic mulls the morrow
Over and again
And then again
And then again
And then again again

She weighs the sense against the sorrow
And sees the friend she's been
Discerning then
That that won't end
When ending she begins again

The Nature of Man

Each night, as I kneel in conversation,
I talk to a great guy.
He's funny, loving, wise and confident all rolled into one.
He's the kind of guy who's best friends with everyone.
My friend is an artist,
Known throughout the entire universe for his magnificent creations.
His most famous work is a sculpture called "Man."
(You've probably heard of it.)
"Man is a self-portrait.
(Except it's a sculpture, so maybe it's a "self-sculptrait.")
My friend gave his sculpture everything:
Love, happiness, and procreation
Even a beautiful display case called "Earth."
He wanted his sculpture to succeed,
So he gave him all the good things he had,
Making his sculpture beautiful.
Now, if you were doing a self-sculptrait,
Would you make it evil and dark and ugly?
Of course not.
And neither did my friend.
He made it good.
Time and opinions have changed the view of "Man,"
As they do all great works of art.
Many now see "Man" as evil and dark and basically bad.
That's their prerogative,
But, I know the artist
And I know his work,
And "Man" is a masterpiece that will last forever.

Retaliation

Defend against the visciousness
You thought you heard him think
Fight back against the faults he never found
Then thrash against your conscience
For starting all this nonsense
And loose the bitter bands that have you bound

Give sunlight to the hatred
For the looks he never gave
Some water for the words he never said
Then tackle thoughts so spiteful
From a heart that's hurt and prideful
And purge the plots you've planted in your head

Despise the hurt he dealt you
Through the acts he never did
Mull over all the malice you've assumed
Then devastate the worry
For conclusions that you've hurried
And pray before your peace becomes consumed

Retaliate the rumors
That you've heard from down the line
Allow the rage inside to steady sneer
Then conquer such creations
As a true retaliation
And watch the ones who hate you disappear

Handprints

Handprints on the mirror
Handprints on the floor
Handprints on the window
Handprints on the door

Handprints on your glasses
Handprints on your keys
Handprints on computers
Handprints on TVs

Handprints on the pictures
Handprints on display
Sometimes it seems those handprints
Will never wash away

And somehow while you're scrubbing
Their endless finger art
You find those little artists
Leave handprints on your heart

Elitist Defeatist

O, Elitist Defeatist
Thou bleakest of men
Thy woe is completest
When thou needest a friend

Thou entreatest the sweetest
Succeedest and then
Elitist Defeatist
Depletest thou him

On a Stage with No Theater

On a stage with no theater
And no crowd to cheer him on
Just the friendly imaginations
Of the person who he'd like to think he really is
He plays
Entertaining those inside of him
With excuses and an actor's grin
Thinking that he's fooling them
And wondering who he could have been
Could be
But clutching to his fictional reality
The curtain's drawn
The makeup's on
And he has gone so far beyond
Being him
And the non habitual drink will heal the world again

On a stage with no theater
And no lights to be turned on
Just the cheering and ovation
From the darkness of the crowd he thought he knew was his
He plays
Wondering what's inside of him
With shattered views and lowered chin
Struggling to fake a grin
And knowing who he could have been
Could be
And longing for his fictional reality
Forgotten dreams
Afraid it seems
Of the things he could have seen
Afraid to see
Afraid to take the pen in this biography

On a stage with no theater
And no lives that could be changed
Just the ones with reservations
Who smile and nod with fairy tale assuredy
He plays
Entertaining those inside of him
With illusions and an actor's grin
Forgetting that he's fooling them
Forgotten who he could have been
Could be
Just playing for his fictional reality
The curtain's drawn
The makeup's on
And he has gone so far beyond
Being him
And the critics clap their hands and he's a star again

Lashing out in Legions

Lashing out in legions
And lesioning your love
Lost in loathing languished lullabies
Lethal lines to last legitimize
Lonely lover's leveraged little lies

I Long No Longer

I long
I lounge
I long
I lounge
I long
I lounge
I long no longer

I long
I lunge
I long
I lunge
I long
I lunge
I long no longer

Trader

I traded my pen for a mouse
That rouses the louse that's within

I traded my page for a screen
That weans me from dreams I begin

I traded my book for a box
That locks out the clocks of my youth

I traded my life for a job
That mobs me and robs me of truth

A Pet Shop with Peeves

A pet shop with peeves
Often achieves
Record sales figures
With low finance fees
They sell them with ease
As fast as they're born
Customers torn
I feel I should warn
The selection's getting bigger
But don't worry
There's no hurry
No need to mourn

When choosing a peeve
You have to believe
In its good breeding
Champion lines
Produce better whines
As all can perceive
But any old peeve
Will tend to achieve
If it's brought up with proper feeding
If you love them
Any of them
Will thrive guaranteed

And multiple peeves
Always relieves
Those undecided
It's easy to feed
Nourish and knead
Two, three or four
Why not get more?
Peeves by the score?
Just ask the trainers who have tried it
It's fantastic
Swipe the plastic
And the critters are yours

A pet shop with peeves
Rarely achieves
High satisfaction
Don't get me wrong
The market is strong
And sales are unreal
But I can't help but feel
This fabulous deal
Will end in a negative reaction
Loyal furies
Only curry
Favor unreal

Rubber-necker's Revenge

"I drove that stretch," he often said
Then he'd square his shoulders and raise his head
And with a grin relate the tale
Of how he earned his spot in jail

The year was nineteen-ninety-nine
The season spring; the weather fine
The day was over. The work was done
The time had come to have some fun

And so commuting in my car alone
I watched the road but dreamed of home
When up ahead I saw the sight
That ruined my plans that fateful night

The freeway stood an endless still
Of rubber-neckers seeking thrills
Their heads were turned; their wonder fed
The radio said a man was dead

The crash had happened hours before
The mangled steel, the blood and gore
Had long been cleared from off the road
But still the traffic stopped and slowed

And as I watched the hours go by
Whining, wishing, and wondering why
A plan began to formulate
Revenge on those who'd made me late

That line of traffic slowing down
To view the carnage on the ground
Or see a drug bust, or watch a fight
Has never seen a full-moon night

They've never watched the sun go down
They've never seen the lights of town
They've never rolled the windows down
To smell the air or look around

And if I do, it's safe to bet
They'll slow down too in hope to get
A glimpse of what it is I see
Some crime or crash catastrophe

And when they find no wreck or fight
They'll be ticked off and it'll serve them right
For rubber-necking at tragedy
And disregarding majesty'

And so on Monday I drove that route
Windows down and head half out
I watched the sunset fade to blue
And when I slowed the rest did too

They craned their necks and looked around
But never saw the sight I'd found
They crept for miles and miles and miles
With bated breath but fading smiles

On Tuesday I was there again
The center lane and doing ten
And cars were stopping left and right
To see what show I'd found that night

But no one saw the circling hawk
Though plenty stopped and plenty gawked
And still they followed close behind
In hope of seeing someone fined

By Friday folks were pretty mad
They couldn't believe the luck they'd had
They'd leave the office by two or three
But always end up following me

They honked their horns and screamed and cussed
I got the finger from an entire bus
But I just kept on slow then stop
Until some cell phone called the cops

And now I'm here for two to five
Then three more years 'til they let me drive
But when they do I'm going to go
Down that same old road and just as slow

"I drove that stretch," he'd say again
Then he'd cock his head and flash a grin
"And I'll drive it more; just wait and see
They never should have messed with me"

Fantasy Island

The raindrops always brought a change
A transformation
A new beginning
The desolation of the unfinished back yard
Became an Eden
And a tropical paradise
Emerged from the vacant lot next door
Water-slides carved by erosion
Ponds created in the abyss of a footprint
And mountains rose from mounds of dirt
GI Joe, Barbie, even Luke Skywalker
Visited this magical haven
Swimming, surfing
Exploring caves, and building castles
Then the sun would scare away the clouds
And the island would vanish forever
At least until the next rain storm
Now we have a shed and dogs and a nice lawn
But we haven't seen the island for years
People can be blind sometimes
But a child can make magic out of a mud puddle

I'm Sick

I'm sick! I'm sick! I'm sick I say
I doubt I'll live another day
I've got a headache and stomach flu
Oh, can't you see I'm turning blue?
I think my arm is falling off
I've got Strep Throat and Whooping Cough
Pneumonia, Croup, and Chicken Pox
And Athlete's Foot from my old socks
What's that? You say you've got Fugue?
Oh yes! That's right. I've got that too
I've got Giardia from river water
Measles, Mumps, and Osgood-Schlatter
I'm sick! I'm sick! I'm nearly dead
I've got the Hives from toe to head
A chronic case of Tonsilitis
Cancer, Perthes, and Laryngitis
Anemia and Variola
Cirrhosis, Chills, and Granuloma
Oh, can't you see I'm about to die?
Why me? Why me? Oh why? Oh why?
So, you saw the doctor yesterday?
Tell me! Tell me! What'd he say?
You've got a cold and sleep's the key?
Well, for heaven's sake, don't breathe on me!

Tea Cups in Your Mind

Spinning three directions
And all at the same time
Faster when you turn the center wheel
Anxiety the only thing you feel
And dizzily, you wonder what is real

Complications winding
Binding up your mind
Grind against the force centrifugal
Emotions wearing down, becoming dull
Watch the peace get spun out of control

But still continue turning
Burning what's inside
Hide your face and shade your teary eyes
Now take a breath and contemplate the size
To turn the wheel is very rarely wise

Spinning three directions
And all at the same time
Slowing as you cease to turn the wheel
Knowing that it's not that big a deal
And concentrate on things you know are real

Why Old Acquaintances Stay that Way

Do I know you from somewhere?
Oh—I didn't mean
It's just—I think I've seen you here before
You really look familiar
Do you come here oft—I mean
Oh, never mind—I'm just not trying anymore

A Bad Day

I took a day off to feel sorry for myself
And wallow in the misery
I was about to create
I hadn't been depressed for quite a while
And it was high time I had a lousy day
So I penciled one in

When the Giant of Town Takes a Fall

Who could have known all the pain I would feel
As he stumbled and fell from the sky
Who would have thought such a blow it would deal
As he landed from falling so high
Who would have thought that he'd leave such a dent
He was only a man after all
But I was amazed at the tremors it sent
When the giant of town took a fall

Who could have known all the lives it'd affect
All the dreams that would fall with the man
Who would have guessed that he'd dive in effect
As the stuff made its way to the fan
Who could have imagined the mountains it'd make
When Babe wrestled roughly with Paul
But faults will collide and foundations will shake
When the giant of town takes a fall

Who would have thought that so many would see
As he slipped and went tumbling down
Who would have guessed the whole kingdom would be
Selling popcorn and gathered around
Who would have thought that the papers would come
In response to anonymous calls
But I guess it's a story for page number one
When the giant of town takes a fall

Who'll ever know all the tears that were cried
All the sorrows for letting them down
Who could have heard the heart breaking inside
Overpowered by the crash on the ground
Who'll ever know that a giant could feel
So ashamed and incredibly small
And waiting he wonders if wounds ever heal
When the giant of town takes a fall

Colorblind

It's hard to know
That an apple is red
When you have no concept of red
Or color for that matter
It's hard to find
The beauty of a deep blue sky
When blue is just another word
With no meaning
And it's hard to see
The greenness of life
When you lack the muscular strength
To open your eyes

The warming light of the sun
Can burn the eyes
Of those who live underground
And bring more pain than sight
Even those who are used to the light
Have to be eased out of the darkness
And those who live in the sun
Cannot look directly at it
It's too hot

But without its rays
We couldn't grow
We couldn't see
We couldn't live
Nothing could
We enjoy its beauty
Through the everyday miracles that it works
Life, warmth and light
A blooming flower
Unlocking its pedals
To allow more light to enter
Opening up to sights and colors it's never seen before
And showing its new-found happiness
To all who see it grow

But it's hard to see
When your eyes are closed
And it's impossible to smile
When you're squinting

It's Raining Now; God's Crying

Bottle caps and prophylactics
Misusing this place
Disgusting
Disgrace
It's raining now; God's crying

A View from the Sixth Grade

In the good
We found the bad
Flowers, cascades
But made us mad

One in a million
We found dark in light
We were the people
Who started the fight

For hundreds of As
We found one B
For thousands of dogs
We found one flee

Bad, bad, bad
We found a ton
For twelve years of work
One second of fun

Miles of blue sky
We found one cloud
In hours of quiet
One second of loud

People should change
And swallow their pride
And always remember
Look on the bright side

At the Annual Dreamer's Convention

At the annual dreamer's convention
A gathering of talented minds
Rolling their lives
As smoke blinds their eyes
And searching for something to find

Hollow wanting in the air
Fantasy and truth or dare
Acceptance for the love-impaired
An endless game of solitaire

But at the annual dreamer's convention
Hopeless and lonely they've found
Charmed by the dream
Of belonging it seems
A circle of friends on the ground

The Battle of the Blue and the Gray

On the shores of a blood-red river
Deep in the valley of soul
Two armies have come to battle for the promised land
One stands clad in established blue uniforms
Singing the songs of achievement
And hoisting the banner of its goal
The other wears only gray
But stands with as much pride
And contentment as the first
Satisfied with the color of its uniform
And bearing a banner
Only within the hearts of the individuals
In the bombarding light of the daytime
The armies are cordial
Playing cards
And having a good time
But in the silence of the night
They take up arms
And battle for the betterment of the whole
Cannons, and gunfire clash with the sounds of crickets
And rob the dark of its peacefulness
Both armies want what's best for the whole
But unfortunately there is no compromise
And no Appomattox
So the battle rages on
Without prisoners or fatalities
Or a conclusion

Not that Guy

I'm not the guy you think you see
The realization of imagery
The kind of guy I'd like to be
I'm not the guy you see in me

My epidermis fits the mold
And looks like him I'm often told
But underneath it's dark and cold
And far too small to fill the hold

I play the part—at least I try
But the inner me is not that guy
And though I hate myself and wonder why
It doesn't make me more that guy

I'm not the guy you think you see
Though someday I aspire to be
Then he and I will turn to we
And be the guy you see in me

Answers to Everyday Questions

The ominous finger
Of the solid white line
Seductively urges him on
Away from his troubles
Away from himself
Away from the next morning's dawn

And where is he going?
He really can't say
But everything's beautiful there
The sun always shines
Responsibility's lost
He knows that he's going
But where

Living for tomorrow
And dying today
Hoping it will all go his way
Someday

The bright colored billboards
Are his only friends now
He reads them and chuckles with pain
He's made his decision
The tears fill his eyes
He's running away from the game

Down the road is the answer
He doesn't know where
But he's sure he'll be much better off
Can't she see he was hurting?
Can't she see this is best?
Can't she see that it just got
Too tough?

Living for tomorrow
And dying today
Hoping it will all go his way
Someday

Hoping it will all go away
Someday

Home for the Hollidays

I'll be home for Christmas
You can smile for me
I'm home above
With those I love
My friends and family

Christmas Eve will find me
Where I've longed to be
I'll be home for Christmas
And all eternity

Alone on a Bus with the Rest of the World

I'd love to share this emotion
But unfortunately I'm all alone
I'd write it down
But how do you write an emotion?
There's something inside my soul
That's longing to come out in the form of poetry
But all I have is words
Which no one on this crowded bus of strangers
Would understand
Or want to hear
And those who would understand
Are thousands of miles away
Wanting to hear
And needing the emotion
Even the words

Half the people here won't give me the time of day
And the other half don't have it
Meanwhile the rest of the world
Is falling apart
And there's nothing I can do
Because I'm here
And alone
With words and emotions
And no translations

Capturing A Lifetime

Capturing a moment
Is difficult to do
A childhood seems a futile quest
For molding all the memories
Of growing up into
Four stanzas seems impossible at best

Capturing emotion
Is difficult to do
A heart-full seems a most illusive task
For fitting all the feelings
I've felt for you into
Four paragraphs is just too much to ask

I guess that means I'm foolish
For writing as I do
Chasing whims with nothing more than words
With little hope of finding
Those pure and precious few
Without them sounding awkward and absurd

Capturing a lifetime
Is difficult to do
Especially one that's been as full as mine
But still I feel this yearning
To illustrate to you
The person you've created over time

Jelly Beans

A giant bag of jelly beans
I didn't pay a cent
The end would never come, it seemed
I could eat to my content

And so I grabbed a green bean
Then yellow, black and red
Saw my Sis'; thought, "Nah, be mean"
So I squished one on her head

Now on with eating more and more
Purple, blue and white
First one, then two, then three, then four
These would last me for all night

I popped a handful as I thought
"Hmm, maybe I should save—
Look at this bag filled to the top
It will last for days and days"

So here and there a handful
And here and there a trick
I'd chomp on six or seven
While I stuck a few on Rick

What a treasure I had found
Yet one I couldn't keep
I'd drop a couple on the ground
And never give a heap

"Oh well," I thought. "There's plenty more"
Was the attitude I had now
So I ate another three or four
And I fed some to a cow

An endless resource, never gone
A treasure, true and dear
But then I saw I had just one
And I began to shed a tear

"I'll save this one," I thoughtfully sighed
And I really tried to wait
But I broke down in a minute's time
For I had tried to stop too late

So the moral of the story is
In case you haven't seen
It's plain and clear and here it is
Be careful with your beans

Never was the Golden Boy

Never was the golden boy
Despite what others thought
Never had the sparkling smile
Or the solid self esteem

Never was as positive
As others knew I was
Never had the dreamy eyes
Or the chin that wouldn't drop

Never was as proud of me
As others were to know me
Never was that confident
That I was the one they knew

I don't really know where the image started
Or what I did to keep it going
I don't know how I earned such confidence
Or such critical acclaim

Expectations are a scary thing
When you know you have to meet them
And every day I'm humbled
At the man the others see

Never was the golden boy
Probably never will be
But I never want to let them down
And so I keep on trying

Contentment

In prior works
I've written a lot about contentment
And the joy that comes with it
Well, at the risk of contradicting myself
Sometimes the happiest moments in my life
Take place in the absence of contentment
When I'm longing, yearning and striving
For more of something
More happiness?
Possibly
Though at the time I may be completely happy
I still want more
And though I want more
At the time, I'm completely happy
I'm just not content
It's true that some of the
Most depressing times in my life
Also take place in the absence of contentment
When I'm longing, yearning and striving for more
Of not something
But anything
And it's true that this may all change tomorrow
Who knows?
Maybe tomorrow
I'll be happily wanting more
Maybe
I'll be struggling to survive with what I have
Maybe tomorrow
I'll just be content

Happy

I'm happy
Though I don't know why
I'm smiling
So, I guess

I'm happy with the morning sky
The fluffy strangers rolling by
The eastern sunrise in my eye
That happiness suggests

I'm happy
Though the day is new
I'm lightsome
So, I guess

I'm happy with the dawning coup
The cleansing of the morning dew
Accomplishments I've yet to do
That intimate success

I'm happy
Though I don't know why
I'm smiling
So, I guess

I'm happy with another vie
Another turn, another try
Another day—I guess that's why
The sudden happiness

My House

I'm building a house that will last through all time
A house that is sturdy and strong
With rigorous blueprints but casual design
And a feeling where all can belong

The foundation is solid where building begins
And the framework is growing throughout
With plenty of windows so sun can come in
And the glow of our lamps can go out

The roof is ascending with each passing day
From a basement that's endlessly deep
With thickening shingles to keep out the rain
And the snow and the hail and the sleet

The carpet is padded with inches of foam
So it's soft on the knees when you fall
And there're closets for times when you need to call home
And I'm working on taking out walls

There's a heater for warming those cold winter nights
And there's soap for the bruises and scrapes
A spiraling staircase for reaching new heights
And a rod for a fire escape

And when it is finished it's going to be such
That you'll know what this mansion is for
With the christening bottle, the finishing touch
A welcoming matt at the door

The I Convention

Standing beside myself
I gaze with contempt
As I witness the things that I do

Sitting inside myself
I feel like a wimp
A fraud who himself isn't true

On Sunday from soapbox
He tells a great plan
With whistles and chorus and bells

But mid Monday morning
He's once again man
Quite certain he'll wind up in hell

And I in the audience
Stare with disgust
While the I two rows down shouts, "Amen!"

And the I over there
Bows his head full aware
Of mistakes that he's made once again

Sitting beside myself
I offer an arm
For the tears that refuse to be shed

Standing inside myself
I realize the harm
All the things that I shouldn't have said

The I at the pulpit
Lets out a great roar
Campaigning for never again

An I in the audience
Replies, "We want more"
And the I two rows down shouts, "Amen!"

And standing afar
In the corner alone
Is the I that they all want to be

Weeping and waiting
And watching his own
And wondering, "What happened to me?"

Monster

There's a monster in my closet
That's ominous and real
And terrifying far more than I show
With glowing eyes and claws that
Can infiltrate and kill
The happiness inside I've come to know

Some nights I sleep for hours
Days or months or years
Without so much as knowing that he's there
But other nights he cowers
And calculates my fears
To catch me in his snarled and sneaking snare

His fangs are gross illusions
That tear through flesh and bone
To secret chambers hidden once from view
And grasp with false delusions
That somehow seem to clone
And devastate the things I know are true

His breath is poisoned fiction
That flatters, fawns and fibs
Seducing with a slow hypnotic hiss
His gaze is an addiction
His manner glut and glib
His silent roar a pained paralysis

When busyness surrounds me
And occupies my mind
With love and life and lists of things to do
The daylight glowing 'round me
Can make me hard to find
And hide me from his microscopic view

But late at night I see him
When lights have been turned out
And lonely I must wrestle with the dark
I struggle not to be him
To weed his memory out
And battle for my mind and for my heart

And when I think I beat him
I sigh with cold relief
And fortify again for nights to come
I struggle not to weaken
To bolster my belief
And welcome once again the rising sun

There's a monster in my closet
Despite what people say
He's haunting me with choices that I've made
And though I know I cause it
The fear won't go away
Until I grow too big to be afraid

Illuminated Leaves of Green

Illuminated leaves of green
Giving birth to morning
As I wander through a world serene
Passively sojourning

The Masterpiece

A smiley faced sun in the corner
With rays extending
Almost to touch the burnt umber roof
Of a house with two windows and a door
Has been replaced by an azure sky at twilight
Hovering on the mountains
With omnipresent mist

Circular smoke climbing from the chimney
Has changed to cloudy mysteries
Casting shadows on the darkened pine forest
Which once was just a tree
Green and scribbled
On a sparkling paper canvas

Tone, mood and definition
Have replaced a simple pureness
And suddenly the masterpiece
Has developed into art

I don't know when
I stopped drawing my family in every picture
Our house and our dog
Or at least the one I wanted

I don't know when I realized
That if the sun was in the corner
The other corner had to have some shadow
Contrast and three dimensions

The masterpiece which adorned the refrigerator door
Has undergone some changes
And slowly the artist recognizes
How good it really was

Many Great Men

Many great men
Have passed this way before me
Many are yet to come
Can I do it?

Realizing my own mortality
Vulnerability and weakness
I stand somewhere in the middle of everything
Knowing that by realizing
I can overcome
But feeling the thickening fear
That comes with realization
And trembling with doubt
As I estimate the distance
To the footprints of my forefathers

The fear is cold and personal
The doubt is heavy and relentless
I long to shed them both
And leap into the light that is there
If I can only conquer
The next two steps

Deep breath
I'm stepping

Nostalgia

The years of life have come and gone
And I, who once proclaimed
The best of years the one you're on
Have found the statement not withdrawn
But often-times disclaimed

Nostalgia for the days gone by
And thoughts of yesteryear
Have brought at times a lonely sigh
And for a moment closed my eye
To good times that are here

And looking lost on "glory days"
I feel some atrophy
And wonder how the hurried haze
Of grown-up life in grown-up ways
Can match my memory

For memories are tried and true
The joy therein is real
But future ones are made by you
And what you with your present do
Ensuing times to till

The years of life have come and gone
And knowing that they will
Forever forward carry on
I cherish those from which I've drawn
And love those living still

Thursday Night's Hellish Adventure

I went to sleep last night
Because I had nothing better to do
I had visited every room in the house
Thirty or forty times
In hope of inspiration
But there was none
I had hundreds of projects
And nothing to do
And so I searched
I looked longingly into the emptiness
Of the full refrigerator
But I wasn't hungry
No one was home to call
And, fully knowing this fact
I called anyway
Just in case
But there were no miracles
No one was home
No friends
No family
And no relief
I was bored
And alone
And increasingly depressed
So I went to bed
In hope of finding company
Somewhere in my dreams
But no one was there
I couldn't sleep

The Swing

A small wind cools the heat of Memorial Day
A blanket of clouds lingers overhead
The swing on the porch doesn't creak
It sits solemnly still
Silent
A stocking cap and a jacket
Protection from the chill of the near June afternoon
Her expression doesn't change
She sits not because she enjoys the silence
But because there's nothing else to do
She will occupy the double swing forever
Alone
Eighty seven years old
She brought ten children into the world
She's seen one go out
Not that she remembers
Not that she remembers anything
Or anyone
Swinging
Occasionally a visitor
But who is it
It's an uncomfortable thing talking with someone
Whom you should know well
But can't remember at all
And so alone she sits and swings
Swinging, swinging
Swinging

Planner

A bought a dateless planner
To track my heres and theres
But found my nowheres couldn't be postponed
So I cancelled without candor
My some- and anywheres
But left bereft my everywheres alone

I grabbed a crooked straightedge
To pencil in the year
But found my pen was running out of ink
So I scribbled circled signage
That ceased to reappear
But left impressed the paper here, I think

Sailing Away

Standing at the dock
Bon Voyage
Hugs and kisses
How they'll miss us
Sail away

Loading the boat
With eagerness
Waving goodbye
Please don't cry
Sail away

Sail away
With confidence that everything's okay
Knowing that goodbye's the only way
It's just one day
But time is all subjective

Sail away
Knowing that with faith it all works out
Unsure just what this life is all about
Afraid of doubt
Just sail away

Lying in bed
At the end of the day
Holding her hand
Unable to stand
Sail away

Loading the boat
For the trip back home
Your final goodbye
And watching her cry
Sail away

Sail away
With confidence that everything's okay
Knowing that goodbye's the only way
It's just one day
But time is all subjective

Sail way
Knowing that with faith it all works out
Unsure just what this life is all about
Afraid of doubt
Just sail away

Rollercoaster

Rising up
The first bump
On the biggest ride of your life
Ascending
Not comprehending
The heartache and the strife
Just waiting
Anticipating
The good times and the highs
Not fearing
The peak is nearing
And it's there before your eyes
The rollercoaster

Falling
Your stomach calling
As you plummet toward the ground
Descending
Afraid of bending
How quick it turns around
Wheels screeching
Your heart is reaching
As you make a turn and then
Ascending
Not comprehending
But you're going up again
The rollercoaster

Enduring
The oft-occurring
Flat times and the spills
Not ceasing
The speed's increasing
As you conquer higher hills
Comprehending
The ride is ending
Looking back on tears you've cried
But the flying
Out-weighed the crying
And you're glad you rode the ride
The rollercoaster

The roller
Rollercoaster
Bringing smiles and bringing tears
The roller
Rollercoaster
Both creates and conquers fears
When you timber
Just remember
What it felt like up above
Once you ride it
You can't fight it
In the end you'll always love
The rollercoaster

The Race: Part Two

I didn't write the first one
But I'd like to add my part
For I too have watched a runner's race
That touched the author's heart

The boys were small and eager
Their fathers filled with pride
The stands were packed with cheering fans
Each rooting for his side

And then the gun was sounded
The race was under way
The runners pushed with all their might
To try and break away

Each dreamed of running fastest
Of ribbons and of charms
Of crossing first the finish line
And then his father's arms

Each longed to win the trophy
Be the hero of the hour
To be lifted up on shoulders where
The praise of fans would shower

But as they circled farther
One boy strong and sure
Began to pull away a step
And then a little more

He clearly was the fastest
The race was surely won
He only had to keep the pace
The other boys could run

But still he pushed on faster
Completing the first round
About the time the last place boy
Went tumbling to the ground

And then amidst the fanfare
And the cheering and the pleas
The leader stopped to help the boy
Who had fallen to his knees

His reaction was automatic
As without a second thought
He broke as fast as he had launched
When the starter's gun was shot

The crowd could scarce believe it
And confused they wondered why
He stayed to brush the small boy off
As the others ran on by

They screamed "Go on! You'll lose it!"
"If you haven't lost it now"
But the leader took the time to see
If he could help the boy somehow

And when the leader, now in last
Knew his colleague was all right
He turned and ran so very fast
It approached the speed of light

The roaring crowd grew louder
As he made his move again
To think that he could lose such time
And still come back to win

But midway through the pack once more
On the way to take first place
The leader turned to see his friend
Landing roughly on his face

And in a flash spun around
And ran the other way
He pulled the fallen from the ground
And asked, "Are you okay?"

The clumsy boy just nodded
And embarrassed watched his feet
Because of him his faster friend
Was likely to get beat

But the leader said "Don't worry"
"Just forget about the fall"
"The race is what's in front of you"
"We're going to beat them all"

From that time on they were a team
The fast boy and the slow
The leader only jogged the pace
The other boy could go

And side by side they ran the race
Until they neared the end
Then the leader slowed his step a bit
To finish just behind his friend

Another boy crossed finish first
Then a second and a third
But the cheers that met the last toy boys
Were the loudest ever heard

"Don't look back; you've got them"
Cry the voices all around
But then I see the leader stop
To lift his neighbor from the ground

The race is won by winners, true
The quickest to the end
But champions are those who stop
To help a struggling friend

Practical Dreaming

I'm a practical dreamer
Dreaming practical dreams
Lost in my idealistic world come true
Aspiring to worldwide mediocrity
And enjoying the excitement
Of fantasy achieved
I'm a practical dreamer
Dreaming practical dreams
Visions of life and love
Common in their incredibility
And incredible in their plainness
Completely full
Like the joy in seeing them fulfilled
Unending and inspiring
My dreams
My love
My life

Standing on My Head

Standing on my head
Has changed the path I tread

Lying on my shoulder
Has made my dreams grow bolder

Sitting on my butt
Has got me out of ruts

And kneeling on my knees
Has conquered enemies

There's a Man that I See

There's a man that I see
When I look inside of me
Trying to break free and be
With you

It's the man I can be
If you'll put your trust in me
Close your eyes and see
Him too

Talking to Myself

I'm talking to myself
At least a part of me
The part I would be
If I could be
I guess the part I should be

I'm talking to myself
And he's an interesting guy
Though I times I want to cry
When he looks me in the eye
And he makes me answer why
And I really don't know why
But he's still a decent guy

And so I'm talking to myself
And we're having a little scuff
Because he makes it kind of tough
When things are going rough
And I think I've done enough
And he says it's not enough
And so I do more in a huff
Until I've finally done enough
And I feel good and all that stuff
And that really gets my guff

But I'm still talking to myself
Because he knows the things I hide
The foolish pride
The tears I've cried
When I've tried
And when I've only kind of tried
And through it all he sees a side
A different side
That's deep inside

And so I'm talking to myself
To see what he
Would have me be
If I could be
That part of me
Which only he
Can help me see

Out of Silence

Out of the silence
A button is pushed
Tendons tightening
The world fighting
Into the havoc
He's suddenly rushed
Heels grinding
The world binding
The sweat on his brow
The fear in his eyes
He doesn't know what to expect from this life

Both feet on the highway
With no cars in sight
Voices calling
Her heart falling
The cool of the night air
She shivers with fright
She doesn't look back
Afraid she might crack
The wind fills with laughter
She stares at the ring
She doesn't know what the next step will bring

An oblivious world
Spins and spins unaware
Immune to the sweat
Immune to the stare
Waiting for someone to care

Binding us all with its sunshine
Waiting
Intoxicating

From out of the darkness
The mirage of a song
The world crying
A friend dying
We fear revolution
And gravity's strong
It pulls us along

World Traveler

I travel the world
When I'd rather stay home
Mingle with crowds
And feel all alone
Pour empty words
Into pages of poem
Prone to roam

I sleep by myself
In a bed made for two
Busy myself
With nothing to do
Think of myself
By thinking of you
Rue adieu

Two Years

Two years can seem like an eternity
When you're looking from the front
And then suddenly two months are gone
Not that they went like that or anything
(Whatever "that" refers to)
But they're gone
And they did go fairly fast
I guess
But twenty-two months can still seem like an eternity
When it's only been five days
And you're readjusting
And reminded
And looking from the front
With no more hope of reminders
And no more challenge of readjusting
That is once you're adjusted
If you're ever adjusted
And then suddenly two more months are gone
And you're waiting for two more days
And they themselves seem like forever
Let alone the twenty months you've still to go
Nineteen
Another gone
And time is accelerating

A year can seem so short
When you're looking from the front
And standing in the middle
Of what used to be eternity
Wondering where a year has gone
And watching another day slip by
Again and again
Until you've only got two months
And you're looking from behind
On twenty-two that seemed so long
But now are just a moment

Two days can seem so long sometimes
And yet so very small
And wondering if you're front or back
Could take another hour

A Perfect Day to Me

There's a joy coming over the mountain
Coming up and bringing the light
Making everything alright
And every morning it rises
But at night when the silence
Holds hostage the sky
And with bondage blockades what I see
I grovel for guidance
And solemnly sigh
That it's almost been a perfect day to me

There's a hope coming over the mountain
Climbing up and making life new
Shining through the things I do
And every morning it soothes me
But at night when the darkness
Demolishes day
And with chaos contends with the free
I hold to the harvest
And silently say
That it's almost been a perfect day to me

The change in the sky
Like the changes of life
The questioning why
The struggle and strife
My midnight is mourning
It's dark. I can't see
But it's almost been a perfect day to me

There's a light coming over the mountain
Rising up and making things bright
Chasing shadows from the night
And every morning it whitens
But at night when the sorrow
Surrounds starry skies
And with malice maligns my marquis
I talk of tomorrow
And whispering wise
That it's almost been a perfect day to me

Heather by Moonlight

Heather by moonlight
On the side of a hill
When a faint autumn chill is sneaking
Twilight blue leaves
On lavender trees
And nobody sees
Me peaking

Wind singing solo
Piano and coy
The love a boy is dying
Maturity cheers
For those who have ears
But nobody hears
Me sighing

Heather by moonlight
On the side of a hill
Never notice until one evening
Crickets compose
As passers-by doze
And nobody knows
I'm dreaming

Whispering starlight
That giggles and grins
A love that begins
Unending
Nature aware
In the calm quiet air
That something is there
Impending

Heather by moonlight
On the side of a hill
When a voice soft and still
Is calling
The moon and the breeze
The shadows and trees
And nobody sees
Me falling

An Alliterative Message to Matt

I ponder on my parted pal
So dearly deemed and dote-worthy

What wondrous works
What warming words
Want I to wend his way

Not knowing now
The things he thinks
Or does from dawn to dimming
I search to send some semblance of
The lingering love and longing
That harbors up the hollows
Of this humble, halting heart

What works would we
Embrace, enjoy involving
One another
When we could wind
The ticking tocks of time
And find a fleeting flicker
A moment more in maliced mires
Of millennial-maniced minds
To void this vicious vacuum
Of the barriers that bind

What with this wanton wonder
React, regain, retrieve
Call caucuses and cast asunder
The laws that led to leave

Island

I don't know how to tell you
What I've said a thousand times
In language only I can understand
With short and simple statements
Designed to help you find
The dark deserted isle to which I'm banned

I know you must have heard me
And you've always listened well
But somewhere on the way
The words were changed
From desperate cries for comfort
To trite and trivial tales
My message in a bottle rearranged

The code is not encrypted
And the warning not that vague
The desperation not that hard to see
But ignorant indifference
Perpetuates the plague
And says "I love you" as you drift to sea

Flying

Flying
Into in the dark of night
Trying
To get the words just right
Dying
Living a life without you
I'm blue

Knowing
Days will keep rolling on
Keep flowing
Got to keep going on
Growing
Stronger with lies that I tell
So well

Weeping
Tears fall inside my head
Not sleeping
Somehow exhaustion's dead
Keeping
Vigil alone through this night
Of flight

Tell Me Your Worries

Tell me your worries
Your sorrows and fears
And I'll listen and won't say a word

Put your head on my shoulder
And wet it with tears
And I'll love you through problems unheard

Hold my hand without squeezing
Caressing or care
Just a steadiness sure and secure

And I'll never let go
But hold happily there
In the softness of knowing I'm yours

Kiss my lips without violence
Or shortness of breath
Kiss them gentle and soft and in love

And I'll hold you forever
Through life and through death
With your happiness payment enough

Chick Flick

He's a sucker for a love story
An ever after end
Perhaps that helps explain the trend
Of female flavored friends
Perhaps that's why in romance
He never could succeed
And never was a woman's want
But oft a woman's need
Perhaps that's why they loved him
Like the brother they'd never had
And looked on him as someone sound
And solid like a dad
Sensitive and caring
Comfortable and strong
Perhaps his nice guy image
Was the thing that did him wrong
Perhaps if he were colder
More selfish, or obtuse
His arms would not be solely used
To comfort past abuse
His heart would not be broken
For those he'd never love
His evenings wouldn't turn to night
With only memories of
The future he could offer
The love that he could give
If female views of chivalry
Did not insist he live
Alone with all the fan mail
Of women's confidence
Extolling endless struggles
With the grass across the fence

If the Situation were Different

If the situation were different
I could tell you how much I love you
And not have to worry
About you loving me back

If I weren't who it says I am
I could show you the admiration
That has grown inside my heart
Since I noticed who you are
And who you could become

With another name and wardrobe
I could dance with you till day break
Share a soft and simple sunrise
And exhaust the hours in between
With casual conversation
As a friend and nothing more

But as hard as I try not to
I can't help but understand
That the person who I am right now
Is the one that I should be

And so I give you glimpses
In hopes that you will save them
Until the situation changes
And I can share the way I feel

Until then, I hope you realize
That behind this plastic title
Is an unofficial person
Who's arms have longed to hug you
And who'd love to be your friend

I'd Like to Take You by the Hand

I'd like to take you by the hand
Show you how I've learned to stand
Go with you to distant lands
I'd like to take you by the hand

I'd like to share a smile with you
Walk an extra mile with you
Sit and talk a while with you
I'd like to share a smile with you

I'd like to sing a song for you
Struggle and be strong for you
Watch life roll along for you
Just sing my little song for you

I'd like to take my time with you
Let the clock unwind with you
Share a secret rhyme with you
I'd like to take my time with you

I'd like to take you by the hand
Follow footsteps in the sand
See the simple somehow grand
I'd like to take you be the hand

Atlantis

Her eyes are like the ocean
Both in color and in form
Silent emerald waters
Glistening in the sunshine
And entrancing in the moonlight
Glassy, hollow
Pools of stillness
Emotion and love
Eyes just moist enough to drown in
Green and clear
Transparent windows
Allowing, for those close enough
An insight to the soul
Oh to be enveloped
Consumed and suffocated
By the pressures of the deep
To dive below the caution
And unsurety
To drown
With no desire for air
No panic
And no fear
Just a peaceful filling of the insides

I Miss You Most in Moments

I miss you in the morning
When she takes me for the day
And keeps me late for meetings
When I just can't break away

I miss you more at lunchtime
When I go on dates with her
But I miss you most in moments
When I see the way we were

I miss you on the weekend
When we run from here to there
And give our time to lovers
For whom we've never cared

I miss you in the minutes
When I find my schedule free
But I miss you most on evenings
When you're lying next to me

Contact without touching
And sleep without the rest
Sharing air between us
But not each other's breath

Knowing that you love me
And having you so near
I never miss you more than
I miss you when you're here

I miss you in the winter
When he woos you for a while
With words of whispered wanting
Full of gall and guiltless guile

I miss you in the springtime
When the world begins anew
But I miss you most in moments
When I wish that we could too

I miss you in the summer
When waken hours are long
And sunshine seems to linger
Its courtship to prolong

I miss you in the autumn
When winter's in the air
But I miss you most severely
In seasons that we share

Love without affection
And dreams without the drive
Sharing life between us
But not each other's lives

Knowing that I love you
And having you so near
I never miss you more than
I miss you when you're here

Exotic Enough for My Taste

Okay, it's a sandbox; not a tropical shore
And a pool; not a distant lagoon
And it's nowhere exotic. And we've been there before
It's just the backyard in the moon
But there's that look in her eye
And that beautiful sigh
And that cute little smile on you face
And holding her hand
As we walk through the sand
Is exotic enough for my taste

So it's the neighborhood park; not a path through the woods
And the trees are not towering pines
And we're tramping around in our jackets and hoods
And we're strolling and taking our time
But there's that look in her eye
And that beautiful sigh
And that cute little smile on you face
And it rains as we walk
And we grow as we talk
And that's exotic enough for my taste

So we're not on a boat on a lake or a gorge
And we're not on a gulf or a sea
The rocking is just the swing on the porch
And the waves are the wind in the trees
But there's that look in her eye
And that beautiful sigh
And that cute little smile on you face
And we sit and we swing
And we talk about things
And that's exotic enough for my taste

On a cool summer's eve
When a rain's on the breeze
And the clouds are a blanket of gray
Or a star-studded night
With the moon glowing bright
At the end of a long hectic day
There's a oneness that's made
From a break in the shade
And a pause from the world's hurried pace
And spending my life
With my friend and my wife
Is exotic enough for my taste

Come and Go

Come and go
But come again
We've found a friend
Worth earning

Friends of friends
And those they know
Who come and go
Returning

Come and go
But come again
Forget the been
Of being

Been has been
But then you grow
So come and go
Care-freeing

Come and go
But stay a while
Enjoy the style
Of living

Smile for smile
And tales we know
Which come and go
Re-living

Come and go
But come again
We've found a friend
Worth holding

Friends of friends
And those they know
Who come and go
Enfolding

He Told Her that He Loved Her

He told her that he loved her
He said he always would
He said the things you're supposed to say
As often as he should
He gave her flowers and candy
And jewelry by and by
He told her that he loved her
But he never told her why

Deceptive Sincerity

I'm sorry for being so nice
So understanding
And caring
I never meant for you to fall in love
I just wanted to share my life with you
Happiness
Sorrow
And all the conglomerated emotions
Of my young and open heart
To love you unconditionally
But I never meant for you to fall in love
I wish I knew what to do
To ease your pain
But I can't think of anything
That doesn't involve being nice
Or caring
Or sincere
So I'll just say I'm sorry
I never meant for you to fall in love

Evenings Out without You

Evenings out without you
More than evenings in within
Have taught me all about you
And the person I was then

But evenings out within you
Just like evenings in without
Are nights that can't continue
As I gloom and gad about

Knowing now the things you knew
Seeing what you saw
Wondering what I wouldn't do
To show to you
The person who

Through evenings out without you
More than evenings in within
Has found himself throughout you
In a life that could have been

Knowing now the things you knew
Seeing what you saw
Wondering how I'll make it through
A life or two
Of evenings without you

Two Weeks to Live

The liquid form of happiness
Has filled my lungs
And caused a pneumonia
That can never be cured
Each breath grows increasingly
Larger than the last
Each sends a surge
Of icy coldness throughout my insides
Filling every muscle with excitement
Until it's ready to explode
And allowing each to experience
A warming relaxation
That creeps in
And soothes the heart
The mind and soul
Until with a glance
The process repeats itself
And once again I'm swept away
In a blissful asthmatic heart attack
No doctor can slow the pulse
Nor take away the thickened blood
That is pushing through my veins
And Chemotherapy won't touch
The cancerous joy
That is eating away my insides
And spreading to my mouth and eyes
Revealing to all
The fullness of my condition
It's too late
And I'm afraid there's nothing they can do
It's just a matter of time

Goodbye in Seven Lines

Seven lines to say goodbye
And knowing that the world goes on
Wondering how and when and why
But seeing what's beyond

Sullen smiles to signify
Seven lines are drawing nigh
Seven lines to say goodbye

Five Years Ago on Friday

Ten years ago on Friday
I told you who I was
And hoped that you would see more than I said

Ten years ago on Friday
My life was changed because
We hadn't learned to love each other yet

Nine years ago on Friday
You showed me who you were
And still I feel expressions that you wore

Nine years ago on Friday
My life became a blur
With clarity I'd never known before

Eight years ago on Friday
You kissed me and I knew
That I could never live outside those eyes

Eight years ago on Friday
We kissed goodbye—it's true
But shook on finding future fond goodbyes

Five years ago on Friday
I asked you for your life
And all the lives that after it would be

Five years ago on Friday
My dream became my wife
And life became a dream it seems to me

Five years ago on Friday
I held you in my hand
And watched you cry my endless happy tears

Forever years from Friday
I'll count the grains of sand
And reminisce on endless happy years

Aluminum

They say it's aluminum
But I have to disagree
It's more like tungsten-carbide
Or titanium to me

They call it aluminum
But I don't think that it's true
The feelings that I feel today
Are platinum for you

I refuse to acknowledge
The makers of years
Authority on emblems
Of time

I don't have to celebrate
Foil-flimsy smears
Or apply the descriptions
Assigned

Who are they to decide
What we call what we've made
Or determine the symbol
Of us

Their logos can't capture
The unyielding braid
Of friendship, and passion
And trust

So it may be aluminum
To those who make decrees
But you and I will always be
A diamond to me

I Loved You When I Met You

I loved you when I met you
I knew I always would

I loved you when I met you
Though I never understood

I loved you when I met you
You can't imagine how

I loved you when I met you
But I really love you now

I don't believe my love has changed
I don't think that it's grown
It hasn't even rearranged
Or become better known

The love I felt while still a youth
Has matured a bit perhaps
But honestly I think the truth
Is found in memory lapse

I'm constantly reminded
Of the feelings of that day
And still with every thought of you
My breath gets caught away

The love I felt when first we met
Remains the love I feel
And though I know I don't forget
I'm awed to find it real

I loved you when I met you
I love you still today

I loved you when I met you
More or less I cannot say

I loved you when I met you
You can't imagine how

I loved you when I met you
But I really love you now

Choose Your Own Adventure

She's just a girl from the pages of yesterday
Re-emerging here from time gone by
Showing up to throw a little plot twist in the way
Allusioning the tears that filled my eyes

And the story goes on
It's the book of life

She's just a girl from the pages of yesterday
Echoing events of long ago
Ironic of the things that I used to want to say
Symbolic of the things I used to know

And the story goes on
It's the book of life

She's just a girl from the pages of yesterday
The one I saw as more than just a friend
Resolving that she's always felt exactly the same way
Here to tie up more than just loose ends

And the story goes on
It's the book of life

She's just a girl from the pages of yesterday
Foreshadowing the joy that's still to come
Bringing themes of hope and trust and love along the way
Close the book and start on chapter one

And the story goes on
It's the book of life

Relationships 101

I have the box still tucked away
And the notes that are inside
From a lady friend of yesterday
I guess I don't know why

I don't keep it because I love her still
I'm not living in the past
In retrospect, I somehow feel
I knew it wouldn't last

I guess I keep it because it holds
The good times that we shared
The memories of days of old
And words that showed she cared

It reminds me of the things I said
The things I thought I meant
And the happiness I often read
Within those notes she sent

It reminds me of the pain I felt
When I knew we had to part
And the devastating blow it dealt
When I watched me break her heart

But over time I've come to see
The precedent we set
The wisdom found in memory
Has silenced the regret

And looking back I feel okay
I'm thankful for the ride
So I have the box still tucked away
And the notes that are inside

Always

You say you'll always love me
I say I love you too
But I guess that's not exactly the same thing
For I will always love you
And know that you love me
But there's a difference that needs distinguishing

Your always is forever
My love is for the now
That doesn't mean that it will go away
I just lack the skill and know-how
To contemplate forever
When I'm awe-struck with the love I feel today

Occasionally

Occasionally you meet someone
Who you've known forever
Introductions are made
Souls collide
Laughter, song and wonder
Fill your days to overflowing
The peace of war fills your heart
Your mind, you soul
You are trapped in a paradise
With no wish to escape
The comfort of confusion
The confusion of comfort
You can trade it all
For what's behind door number three
But what is behind that door?
Is the world really round?
Or do these next few steps
Lead me into a vacuum of unemotional nothingness?
Is it all a game?
And, if so, how do I win?
What is behind that door?

In The Mansions of My Father

In the mansions of my father
I learned to be a man
To stand up strong; to strive and struggle through
To take the time; to bother
To conquer all I can
To do my best in everything I do

In the mansions of my father
I learned to be a boy
To find the joy of living void of fear
To take the time; to bother
To genially enjoy
The multifarious moments that I'm here

In the mansions of my father
I learned to be a spouse
To love in ways I never understood
To take the time; to bother
To hallow home and house
To see my wife as life's most gracious good

In the mansions of my father
I learned to be a dad
To tickle, tease, and teach with tenderness
To take the time; to bother
To treasure what I had
To bolster, brighten, build, believe, and bless

In the mansions of my Father
There is a place prepared
And someday, if I live the things I learned
In the mansions of my father
The love my parents shared
Will maybe in some small way be returned

The Reality of Transfers

A sweetly solemn sense of parting
Fills the world with hesitation
Heavy heartfelt memories
Of my life the last eight hours
So fun, so free
So full of life
Ending
As all things
In the hands of man must do
And landing in the hands of God
For an undetermined time of separation
A memory longing to be more
And hope fighting through the ominous insecurity
Of goodbyes to those you love
A shaking hand
A trembling heart
A faith filled smile of understanding
Admiration and love
The beautifully painful knowledge
Of your own uncertainty
And the happiness
Of living a day that's worth it
There will always be tomorrows
And trusting
I smile and say goodbye

Just Love Me Along

See me inside
See who I'm really trying to be
Just close your eyes
And see the inner side of me
Know that I try
Know that there's so much more to see
Just give me time
Please don't give up on me
Just love me along

Give me your hand
Holding it tight I'll make it through
Just let me stand
Just let me learn from things I do
Please know I can
Please let me be in love with you
See through this man
See all the things that you could do
Just love me along

See me inside
See who I'm really trying to be
In me confide
In me you'll find a certainty
Just close your eyes
Just give me time and you will see
Just you and I
Building our own eternity
Just love me along

Where's the Justice?

The reason I doubt the justice of heaven:
On a scale of one to ten, my wife is an eleven

Nothing Leaves the Rock

From just a few yards away
The lights cluster
Into an enormous honeycomb
Full of the pure sweetness of life
The view of a God
An unframed work of art
Stretching endlessly
And nothing leaves the rock
Hearts are exchanged
Without the loss of blood
The warm, red drink of life is shared
Without the use of blades
The words are often silent
Singing in harmony with the comfort of the wind
Silent, delicate, desperate, and determined
And nothing leaves the rock
No Boy Scout could untie
The knot of lives entranced
In the cool of the darkened air
No evil could invade
The oneness that evolves
On the unmarred page of love
A covenant is made
An eternity is paved
And everything leaves the rock

Saying Goodbye

I'm torn
Part of me is going to miss you
That part is uncomfortable with change
Afraid of progression
Enjoying contentment
Part of me is glad you're gone
That part is founded in confidence
Always looking for a chance to move on
Enjoying enjoyment
That part is in love
The first part is a thinker
A questioner
Full of wonder and fear
Sometimes I think he thinks too much
The second part is a doer
A mover
Full of excitement and life
Sometimes I think he thinks too little
I don't know what to think
I don't know what to feel
All I know is that you're gone
Forever
So I guess this is goodbye

The Sean Holliday Overture

That small red object on my head
Is no apple
Though it does have seeds
And one day those seeds
Will grow a creation
Far more beautiful than any tree
And bring forth fruit
More desirable than any other
It's not an apple
It's my heart
Oh—no—it's okay
I put it there
I wanted you to see it
And don't worry
It's still beating
Probably faster than it ever has
I put it there
Because it felt so good
And I wanted to share it with you
Why?
Because I like you
Love you
I know there're a lot of archers out there
Besides Cupid
Who would miss my heart
And shoot my head
And there're probably a few
Who would shoot my heart
With something other than love
But I'll take my chances
Because
1: My heart's comfortable on my head
It needs the fresh air
And 2:
I have faith in the archer

Semblance

Whenever I try to say it
With rhythm, rhyme and word
There's nothing there
But shallow air
And verse that sounds absurd

Injustice in the writing
Inadequate and small
A feeble try
To tell you why
But I just can't list it all

I try in vain to show it
But I simply don't know how
To reciprocate
A trust so great
With what I'm writing now

And in a thousand stanzas
These words could never lend
A semblance of
The joy and love
I find in you, my friend

And so the lines grow longer
And weaker at the end
And being done
I've just begun
Because I've failed again

Melted Together

Your soul is my soul
Your flesh is my flesh
Your mind and my mind are combined
We've melted together
And now we're a mess
Our insides are all intertwined

My hands are your hands
My feet are your feet
My heart and your heart beat as one
We've melted together
And now it's complete
The merging cannot be undone

We're stuck with each other
Forever I suppose
And I guess I deserved what I got
We've melted together
'Cause that's how it goes
When you mingle with something so hot.

Love

As softly falls the loveliness
The dreams all stirred in one
It sneaks up with a tenderness
The warmth outlasts the sun

It's amazing now the sights we see
With the change the lenses cause
Our minds are opened but hardly free
The world is placed on pause

As softly falls the loveliness
As soft as falling snow
The love of life — an eagerness
The love of one — a glow

The lenses lead us down the path
Whatever path we would
Blinders from the hate and wrath
Portals to the good

As softly falls the loveliness
The glasses shade the wrong
Our hearts are filled with happiness
Our souls are filled with song

Vision is perfect thing
When we've got our glasses on
The lens we wear determines things
It sparks a new day's dawn

As softly falls the loveliness
As soft as fading light
Our world is filled with holiness
And peace invades our night

Look at Tomorrow

Look at tomorrow today
It can seem far away
Still knowing it's there
Is the fear that we fear
Through the dark of the forthcoming night
There's light

Tears fall in expectation
It seems we've just begun
There's a vagueness
A haze all around us
The sun it is setting
The fear of forgetting

Night invades the world
Blinding our eyes
Withholding truth
Darkened skies
Why has the sun vanished
From our lives?

Hear the cries
Of our friends
All days must end
Just one more night
Before the closing of lives
But I see tomorrow
In your eyes
Please don't cry

Look at tomorrow today
It can seem far away
The orange sky is fading to night
Have we learned wrong from right?
The fear of the sunset
And light isn't gone yet

Tomorrow's horizons
A goal to shed light on
The world keeps on turning
Our poor hearts are yearning
When darkness has conquered the sky
There's light
In your eyes

Light is here today
It's in your smile
It shows the way
To the skies
And I see tomorrow
In your eyes
Sparking life

Hope is going forth
It conquers night
It conquers dark
It will rise
And I see tomorrow
In your eyes
In your eyes

Look at tomorrow today
It can seem far away

My Wife Thinks I'm Hot

My wife thinks I'm hot
Which doesn't make sense
But—I guess—who am I to complain?
The fact that I'm not—
More a frog than a prince—
I don't feel the need to explain

They say that a marriage
Is founded on trust
And—I guess—to a point that is true
But myself to disparage
Though the slight may be just
Is something I've no plans to do

I may be deceiving
The woman I love
But ignorance it's said can be bliss
And to leave her believing
In fantasies of—
Is only a little amiss

And though she's misguided
Naïve and misled
And despite her delusional views
If perceptions were righted
And she saw what she'd wed
It would ruin my delicate ruse

So my wife thinks I'm hot
And I know it's not true
And—I guess—you could say I'm a liar
But one thing I'm not
Is dumb enough to
Extinguish this goddess' fire

Can You Lift Your Voice up to the Clouds

Can you lift your voice up to the clouds
And harmonize your heartache
When the sky is blue with grayness
And sings a lonely song?
Do they listen?

Are there cirrus ears to hear you
Or stratus arms to hold you
When heaven hangs a heavy head
And slumps its saddened shoulders?
Do they nod with understanding?
Do they hear the words you cry?

Are cumulus smiles contagious
When you lie back
And know who made them?
Do they answer with assurance?
Do they speak in silent psalms?
Do you listen?

Can you lift your voice up to the clouds
And sense a stilling softness
When telestial time is ticking
And you feel you're left behind?
Do they know?

The Binding

Cords bound him
And burned the flesh
Imaginary in their substance
But eternal in their truth
Pulled tight by the honor
With which they were tied
They stood for justice
As the world was robbed
And held him witness
Until he shut his eyes
And withdrew the support of his soul
Helpless with his ultimate power
A plea—and the chords dug in
A tear—and they tightened more
Wisdom overruled emotion
And omniscience omnipotence
There was nothing to do
But wait
And know

Un-nameable

Webster could not define this emotion
He couldn't put a definition
On the conglomerated vacuum
Of fear and rage
Loneliness and sorrow
The blindfolded search
For anything of substance
Anything in the dictionary
Why are there no words?
Why do I feel like a finger-painting
With no picture
No meaning
Not even a name?
Why
What a stupid question
Or is it a question at all?
I don't want an answer
I just want relief
Relief from the undefinable emotion

A Walk in the Rain

The clouds move in
The rain falls down
Sparking life
Ushering in the smell of rain
A fresh invigorating aroma
Full of hope
Full of life
It fills my lungs
It fills my soul
The world is mine
The rain falls down
Sparking life
Creating worlds
Allowing the earth to breathe
Fantasy invades reality
The world is mine
The rain falls down
Sparking life
Spongy ground puts a spring in my step
Shiny, moist droplets drip from every leaf
Leaves hold on
Yearning for one last taste
Of the sweetness of life
Which only the rain can bring
The air is open and free
No one else is around
The world is mine
As the rain falls down

Bad Guy

Pulling on new faces
Like pulling on new clothes
With a passion for the time you're changed
But unsure of what you wear
Cold and hard and ugly
Reflections of all the things you've tried to overcome
Or have never even known
Brought from somewhere, nowhere
And displayed as always there

Pulling on emotions
Like pulling on a storm
With excitement for the thundered rain
But a fear of getting soaked
Gray and weird and wondering
Perceptions of all the things you've seen through frightened fog
And have tried to comprehend
To pierce the night with lightning
In a hollow, icy air

Mulling over questions
Like mulling over fears
With foreboding for the answers found
But a need to understand
Deep and dark and searching
Reflections of all the things you've never dared to ask
Or just didn't want to know
To give the answers clearly
By the way you hold your eyes

Pulling on the bad times
Like pulling on the good
With a love for those who've hated you
And esteem for those who've loved
Strange and thick and charming
Reflections of all the ones who've watched and understood
Or have hoped they never will
To fill the room with pleasure
As they cheer and watch you die

Stumbling on The Rain

I bumped into the evening
And stumbled on the rain
Aware that it had rained all day
I was taken by surprise
I had watched it from the window
But I hadn't touched the smell
I hadn't seen the far off sounds
Of puddles playing poker
Or heard the glistening sidewalk
Whisper limericks to my toes

I halted just a moment
To realize what I knew
To breathe the trickling echoes in
And taste the drunken air
I had viewed it from my shelter
But I hadn't seen the storm
I hadn't felt the darkened clouds
Or touched the chanting thunder
Or heard the distant rainbow
Sprinkle droplets on my tongue

Limerick

My lips got burned to a crisp
So, now, I don't breathe; I just wisp
If you hear me talk
You'd better not mock
'Cause for once in my life I don't lisp

Anti-Buddhist Christian Diatribes Exude Fallacy

A Buddhist Church doesn't exactly forge good humor in Jackson
Klansmen level much nastiness on prelates
Quaint religions silence their unwarranted vexation
With xenophobic yokel zealots

What Are You Willing to Give

"What are you willing to give?" he asked
And I answered, "All I've got"
"It will take much more that that," he chuckled
And I went away confused

"What are you willing to pay?" he asked
"Everything," I said
"I'm afraid that's not enough," he sighed
And I went away irate

Again he asked my willingness
And again I answered all
Again he gently shook his head
And I went away in tears

"What are you willing to give?" he asked
"All I've got and more"
And accepting my humble plea for help
He smiled and let me in

What I Want

I want to cry
I also want to clench my fist
And pulverize everything I see
Including and especially myself
I want to play some music
Go to sleep
And forget I'm even writing this pathetic poem
I want
I don't know what I want

Weeding it Out

Twisted thoughts of wrath and rage
Hauntingly ominous
Scary
Despised because they're there
And strengthened by the disgust
Held in by love and discouraged desire
Trapped by the cause for which they are fighting
Struggling to break free
But demanding to remain
Bringing nothing but fatalities
To a war-torn soul
Tears fall
Laced with humility and heartache
Fists pound
With anger and despair
Bruising only fleshy walls
That hold them prisoner
Helpless and alone
In a crowded cell of principle
Fingers clench
Striving to let go
Truth shouts
Pleading to be held
Hearts fall to their knees
And peace talks begin

Witty Little Ditty

I wanted to write a short little ditty
But wasn't quite sure what one was
Must a ditty be witty?
Because if it does
A short little ditty this was

Empty

Empty
Like the page before I wrote
Full of nothing
Bursting at the seams
With no room left for something
Or everything
Or anything
But nothingness
To fill the in-betweens

Eternity for Men

My inability to imagine eternity
Will be my downfall
If I try to hard to imagine it
But maybe
If I tuck it away in my head
As one of those you know
But only think about one life at a time
Then someday
I won't have to imagine

Orion

The imitation lights of the world
Sometimes filter out
The natural glow of the heavens
Creating a haze
Of neon and fluorine
That blinds the human eye
But, just a few steps back from the glare
Allows your pupils to adjust
And the universe to open
There in the darkness
Everything is clear

It's here that you find him
Standing boldly for all to see
Illuminating and enlightening
The big brother to the world
Watching over the universe
With bow drawn back
Ready to battle any universal enemy

He's there
Up where the sky is clearer
Above the fog of disappointment
And the smog of competition
Above the lights of the world
And beyond the glare
I guess some things are easier to see in the dark

Indigestion

Darkness swallows the earth
The ulcerous acids of evil
Begin the digestion process
A war beneath the crust
Sheltered by a rib cage of blindness
A tearful eye
A burning heart
How do you spell relief?

Falling Star

It must have been so hard for him
Always shining, always bright
Alone up in the heavens
To illuminate the night
With so much darkened space up there
To fill with just his light
It must have been so tiring
Always shining, always bright

It must have been so burdensome
For such a little star
To sparkle so immensely
That his light could reach so far
To hang there night and night again
And let his light so shine
I can see how that would be too much
After such a lengthy time

And the funny thing about it
And the irony of it all
Is that we feel such happiness
As we watch a star that falls
And though I'm sure it's tiring
To shine so long and bright
Perhaps it's more in sacrifice
That they give their final light

It must have been so hard for him
To hang there through the years
And shine his little heart out
When he saw the world in tears
Perhaps his fall was nothing more
Than a final little try
To fill some heart with peace and joy
As he dove and waved goodbye

For Just a Little While

I'm making myself love you
For just a little while
To justify the things I have to do
The words that have to whisper
The silly sort of smile
The eyes that have to suffer over you

The lips that have to linger
The hands that have to hope
To hold you how they hold the hands of her
And when the evening's over
The kid who has to cope
With watching from within the way we were

The feelings are fictitious
Made up to mar my mind
And trick me into treating them as true
But manufactured moments
Just like the natural kind
Can find a way to stay inside of you

So I'm making myself love you
For just a little while
To live the lives of lovers others lived
But privately I ponder
And passively compile
The pureness of a love that's positive

Fresh-Cut Flowers

Fresh-cut flowers
Still have life
They still have color
And beauty
Some are big and boisterous
Overflowing with excitement
Some are small and fragile
Living only for themselves
All are young
And fresh
Exploring their first spring
Flowers
Sometimes the most beautiful
Are covered with thorns
Protection from whatever may be out there
Petals stretching skyward
Reaching out
For sunlight
Rain
Any form of nourishment
Desperately trying to photosynthesize
To carry on
Fighting against the
Withering nothingness of mediocrity
Searching for the sun

Daisies and dandelions
Lilies and lilacs
Blossoms by the dozen
Variety innumerable
With wires and ribbons
Patience and love
They can all be brought together
Unified and inspired
Forming a bouquet of life
Of love
Of memories
Reflective of the Florist
And reflective of the future
Fresh-cut flowers
Still have life
They still have color
And beauty
Fresh-cut flowers
Still have growth

Thoughts in the Garden

Favorite place
Friendly place
The stars of ancient skies

Lovely place
Lonely place
With endless watching eyes

Crying place
Crowded place
And whisper what it's for

Charming place
Changing place
Often here before

Scarlet place
Scary place
Hesitation in the air

Purging place
Pleading place
With doubts you cannot share

Haunting place
Holy place
And breath you can't inhale

Blameless place
Bleeding place
But love and faith prevail

Favorite place
Friendly place
With those you've always known

Pleasant place
Pretty place
And still you sit alone

Quiet place
Quenching place
And whisper who it's for

Wondrous place
Waiting place
Often here before

Pondering

Pondering
Not about anything in particular
Just pondering the thought
That I have nothing to ponder
And finding myself lost and entranced
In the depth of the subject
Pondering to be ponderous
Wondering what I should wonder
Searching for something to search for
And finding there's nothing to find
Just pondering

Holy Night in Early Spring

Darkened stable full of light
Dawning in the heart of night
Home to cattle
Home to kings
Home to hope for every thing

Silent night in early spring
Hear the choirs of angels sing
Songs of rapture
Tales of joy
Reverence for the newborn boy

Born of parents born of love
Born below of Him above
Born to perish
Born to live
Born to take that He might give

Born to die that we might live
A gift that only He could give
Life eternal
Life of joy
Bought with that small baby boy

Violent night in early spring
Hear the storms of thunder ring
Songs of mourning
Days of night
Quenching evil's appetite

Darkened tomb of radiant light
Empty with the passing night
Home to heartache
Home to glee
Home to hope and history

Therefore I Am

I ceased to be the other day
When a thought I thought got caught away
And left me thoughtless for?I'd say
At least a moment anyway

They say that thinking one becomes
That thought is that that matters once
The matter of one's matter's done
And one begins to be begun

And if that's true I wonder then
Do existent instants tend to end
When thinking thins and blanks begin
To block the thought from minds of men

Do misty moments void of thought
Suggest unless a thought is sought
The thoughtless thinker fades to naught
And withers wayward lot by lot

Or is the saying simply that
A pithy myth with iffy fact
Extracting that that is abstract
To actuate awaiting acts

Silence

My mind is lost in endless wonder
I could speak but my mouth is too heavy
It would be terribly wrong to ruin the silence now
Everyone around me is talking
Meaningless statements
Small talk; very small
The fan above my head clicks a steady heartbeat
I can hear the air moving
I can hear the soft "tick tock"
Of the ancient wooden clock on the wall
I can hear the scratch of my pencil lead
Taking the virginity of this page
And yet leaving it with so much more
A dog barks
A car thunders by
But my mind is not in this room
It's on a beach, listening to the waves roll in
It's in a forest, hearing the wind
Listening to it fight its way through the branches
Of the powerful trees
It's on the roof top, gazing at the stars
And humming along with the songs of the crickets
My mind is not in this room
It's too busy enjoying the silence

Stage Kiss

There's a love I left when I was younger
Standing lonely in my mind
And every now and then I hunger
For the love I left behind

Oh if I could just caress her
Find some way to meet again
Let her know how much I miss her
Live the love I lived back then

There's a love I left when I was younger
Before life made a man of me
And sometimes late at night I hunger
For the boy I used to be

Oh if I could just caress her
One more time—I'd never leave
But reminiscing I remember
The mysteries of make-believe

There's a love I left when I was younger
And one day I'll find her again
Then I'll feed this hollow hunger
That will follow me till then

Advice from the Non-Bulimic

I'm hungry
I just ate, but it only made me more hungry
My stomach is yearning for nourishment
It's growling for the sweet taste of food
Let's face it—I love eating
I love it
And even though I just ate
It wasn't enough
It's never enough
I wish my mouth were bigger
So I could increase the velocity of my intake
It's overwhelming
So much food and so little time
I'm just so hungry
I want to eat
And then have seconds—and thirds
The more I eat, the more I starve
The more I starve, the more I eat

Try some! You'll love it!
Taste this! It's delicious!
And the recipe is so simple

You there, don't!
How could you give up that beautiful morsel
Without fully digesting it?

And, you, eat something!
There's an entire feast sitting in front of you
Eat!

Don't be afraid of getting fat
Let your lard so shine
Eat something!
Before you wither away
How can you ignore it?
Why can't you see the beauty
The necessity of nourishment?

Stop playing with your food!

Made in the USA
Charleston, SC
19 December 2016